READING PYTHON

With over 249 python questions & answer

Compiled by oluwasegun Aina

Copyright © 2023 by Oluwasegun Aina

ANSWERS COMES FIRST,

QUESTIONS START

FROM PAGE 66

ANSWERS

1. Answer: Python is a high-level, interpreted programming language known for its simplicity and readability.

2. Answer: PEP 8 is a style guide for Python code that provides guidelines on how to format code for better readability.

3. Answer: A Python package is a collection of modules that can be used to organize and distribute Python code.

4. Answer: A list is mutable, meaning its elements can be changed, added, or removed. A tuple is immutable, meaning its

elements cannot be modified once it is created.

5. Answer: A lambda function is an anonymous function in Python that can be defined using the lambda keyword.

6. Answer: The if __name__ == "__main__" statement allows a module to be executed as a script if it is run directly, but not if it is imported as a module.

7. Answer: The == operator compares the values of two objects, while the is operator compares the identity of two objects.

8. Answer: You can copy an object in Python using the copy module or by using slicing.

9. Answer: The __init__ method is a special method in Python classes that is automatically called when a new instance of the class is created. It is used to initialize the attributes of the object.

10.   Answer: A shallow copy creates a new object with references to the original object's elements, while a deep copy creates a completely independent copy of the original object and its elements.

11.   Answer: The super() function is used to call a method from the parent class in a subclass.

12.   Answer: Exceptions can be handled in Python using the try,

except, else, and finally keywords.

13.   Answer: A generator function is a special type of function that returns an iterator, which can be iterated over using a for loop.

14.   Answer: The Global Interpreter Lock is a mechanism in CPython (the reference implementation of Python) that allows only one thread to execute Python bytecode at a time.

15.   Answer: The yield keyword is used in generator functions to pause execution and return a value, without terminating the function.

16.   **Answer: Some of the built-in data types in Python include integers, floats, strings, lists, tuples, dictionaries, and sets.**

17.   **Answer: You can open and read a file in Python using the open() function and the file object's read() method.**

18.   **Answer: The with statement is used to ensure that a file or resource is properly closed or released after being used.**

19.   **Answer: The append() method adds a single element to the end of a list, while the extend() method adds multiple elements by appending each one individually.**

20.　　Answer: The append() method adds a single element to the end of a list, while the extend() method adds multiple elements by appending each one individually.

21.　　Answer: The pass statement is a placeholder statement in Python that does nothing. It is used when a statement is required syntactically but no action is needed.

22.　　Answer: You can reverse a string in Python by using slicing with a step value of -1.

23.　　Answer: The range() function is used to generate a sequence of numbers that can be used in loops.

24.   Answer: The break statement is used to exit a loop prematurely.

25.   Answer: The continue statement is used to skip the remaining code in a loop and move to the next iteration.

26.   Answer: A shallow copy of a list creates a new list object that references the same elements as the original list. A deep copy creates a new list object with copies of the original list's elements.

27.   Answer: You can remove duplicate elements from a list in Python by converting it to a set and then back to a list.

28.   Answer: You can find the index of an element in a list using the index() method.

29.   Answer: The join() method is used to concatenate elements of an iterable (such as a list) into a single string, using a specified delimiter.

30.   Answer: The format() method is used to insert values into placeholders in a string.

31.   Answer: The strip() method is used to remove leading and trailing whitespace characters from a string.

32.   Answer: The replace() method is used to replace occurrences of a substring with another substring in a string.

33.   Answer: The split() method is used to split a string into a list of substrings based on a specified delimiter.

34.   Answer: A decorator is a special type of function that can be used to modify the behavior of another function without changing its source code.

35.   Answer: The staticmethod decorator is used to define a static method in a class, which is a method that belongs to the class rather than an instance of the class.

36.   Answer: The classmethod decorator is used to define a class method in a class, which is a method that operates on the

class itself rather than an instance of the class.

37.   Answer: A module is a file containing Python definitions and statements that can be imported and used in other Python programs.

38.   Answer: The __name__ variable is a special variable in Python that stores the name of the current module. When a module is run as a script, its __name__ is set to '__main__'.

39.   Answer: The sys module provides access to some variables used or maintained by the interpreter and functions that interact with the interpreter.

40.   Answer: The os module provides a way of using operating system-dependent functionality in Python programs.

41.   Answer: You can check if a file exists in Python using the os.path.exists() function.

42.   Answer: The pickle module is used for serializing and deserializing Python objects. It can convert objects into a byte stream and vice versa.

43.   Answer: The json module provides methods for working with JSON (JavaScript Object Notation) data, including serialization and deserialization.

44.   Answer: The datetime module provides classes for

working with dates, times, and time intervals in Python.

45.   Answer: The random module provides functions for generating random numbers and performing random selections.

46.   Answer: The time module provides functions for working with time-related functions, such as getting the current time, sleeping, and measuring elapsed time.

47.   Answer: The re module provides functions for working with regular expressions in Python.

48.   Answer: The collections module provides additional data structures and utility functions

beyond what is available in the built-in types.

49.　　Answer: The itertools module provides functions for creating and working with iterators and iterator-related operations.

50.　　Answer: The unittest module provides a framework for writing and running tests in Python.

51.　　Answer: A docstring is a string literal that appears as the first statement in a module, function, class, or method definition. It is used to provide documentation about the object.

52.　　Answer: You can access command-line arguments in

Python using the sys.argv list in the sys module.

53.	Answer: The sys.exit() function is used to exit from Python programs, terminating the script execution.

54.	Answer: The os.path module provides functions for working with file paths and directories in a platform-independent way.

55.	Answer: The os.getcwd() function is used to get the current working directory.

56.	Answer: The os.chdir() function is used to change the current working directory.

57.	Answer: The os.mkdir() function is used to create a new directory.

58.   Answer: The os.rmdir() function is used to remove an empty directory.

59.   Answer: The os.remove() function is used to delete a file.

60.   Answer: The os.rename() function is used to rename a file or directory.

61.   Answer: The os.path.isfile() function is used to check if a given path is a file.

62.   Answer: The os.path.isdir() function is used to check if a given path is a directory.

63.   Answer: The os.path.exists() function is used to check if a given path exists.

64.   Answer: The os.path.join() function is used to join one or

more path components into a single path.

65.   Answer: The os.path.splitext() function is used to split a path into its base name and extension.

66.   Answer: The os.path.dirname() function is used to get the directory name from a given path.

67.   Answer: The os.path.basename() function is used to get the base name of a file or directory from a given path.

68.   Answer: The os.path.getsize() function is used to get the size of a file in bytes.

69. Answer: The os.path.getmtime() function is used to get the last modification time of a file.

70. Answer: The os.environ dictionary provides access to the environment variables of the current process.

71. Answer: The os.path.expanduser() function is used to expand the tilde (~) character to the user's home directory path.

72. Answer: The os.path.expandvars() function is used to expand environment variables in a given path.

73. Answer: The os.path.abspath() function is

used to get the absolute path of a file or directory.

74.   Answer: The os.path.normpath() function is used to normalize a path by collapsing redundant separators and up-level references.

75.   Answer: The os.path.relpath() function is used to get the relative path between two paths.

76.   Answer: The os.path.commonpath() function is used to get the common base path of a set of paths.

77.   Answer: A context manager is an object that defines the methods __enter__() and

__exit__() that allow it to be used with the with statement.

78.   Answer: You can define a context manager in Python by creating a class that implements the __enter__() and __exit__() methods.

79.   Answer: The yield statement in a context manager is used to define the point at which the __enter__() method is executed, and where the context is acquired.

80.   Answer: The __enter__() method is called when entering a context managed block, and it should return the context object.

81.   Answer: The __exit__() method is called when exiting a

context managed block, and it allows for cleanup and exception handling.

82.   Answer: The @contextmanager decorator is a convenient way to create a context manager using a generator function.

83.   Answer: The try statement is used to enclose a block of code that might raise an exception, and it is followed by one or more except or finally clauses.

84.   Answer: The except statement is used to define a block of code that is executed if an exception occurs in the corresponding try block.

85.   Answer: The finally statement is used to define a block of code that is always executed, regardless of whether an exception occurs or not.

86.   Answer: The else statement in a try block is executed if no exceptions occur in the corresponding try block.

87.   Answer: An exception is an event that occurs during the execution of a program that disrupts the normal flow of the program's instructions.

88.   Answer: An error is a mistake or flaw in a program that prevents it from running correctly. Errors can be syntax errors, runtime errors, or logical errors.

89.   Answer: The raise statement is used to explicitly raise an exception.

90.   Answer: The assert statement is used to assert that a certain condition is true, and if it is not, an AssertionError exception is raised.

91.   Answer: An iterator is an object that implements the __iter__() and __next__() methods and represents a stream of data that can be iterated over.

92.   Answer: The iter() function is used to create an iterator object from an iterable.

93.   Answer: The next() function is used to get the next item from an iterator.

94.   Answer: The StopIteration exception is raised to signal the end of an iterator.

95.   Answer: A generator is a special type of iterator that is defined using a function and the yield keyword.

96.   Answer: The yield statement is used to define the points at which the generator yields a value to the caller.

97.   Answer: A generator uses the yield statement to suspend and resume its execution, allowing it to produce a sequence of values over time. A regular function returns a single value and then terminates.

98.   Answer: A coroutine is a special type of function that can suspend its execution and transfer control to another coroutine.

99.   Answer: The async keyword is used to define a coroutine function in Python.

100.   Answer: The await keyword is used to suspend the execution of a coroutine until a coroutine or future object completes and returns a result.

101.   Answer: An asynchronous generator is a special type of coroutine that can produce a sequence of values asynchronously.

102.   Answer: The asyncio module provides a framework for writing asynchronous code using coroutines, tasks, and event loops.

103.   Answer: An event loop is the core component of the asyncio module that manages and schedules coroutines and callbacks.

104.   Answer: A task is a subclass of Future that wraps a coroutine and schedules it to run in the event loop.

105.   Answer: A future is an object that represents the result of a computation that may not have completed yet.

106. **Answer: The async with statement is used to define an asynchronous context manager.**

107. **Answer: The async for statement is used to asynchronously iterate over an asynchronous iterable.**

108. **Answer: A thread is a separate flow of execution that can run concurrently with other threads within a single process.**

109. **Answer: The threading module provides a high-level interface for creating and managing threads in Python.**

110. **Answer: The Global Interpreter Lock is a mechanism in CPython (the reference implementation of Python) that**

allows only one thread to execute Python bytecode at a time.

111.   Answer: The threading.Thread class is used to create and manage threads in Python.

112.   Answer: A thread-safe object is an object that can be safely accessed and manipulated by multiple threads without causing data corruption or race conditions.

113.   Answer: A race condition occurs when two or more threads access shared data concurrently, and the final result depends on the relative timing of the thread execution.

114.   Answer: The Lock class in Python threading is used to provide a simple synchronization mechanism to prevent multiple threads from accessing shared data simultaneously.

115.   Answer: The RLock (or reentrant lock) class is a variant of the Lock class that allows a thread to acquire the same lock multiple times without deadlocking.

116.   Answer: The Condition class is used to provide a more advanced synchronization mechanism that allows threads to wait for a specific condition to become true.

117.   Answer: The Event class is used to provide a simple

synchronization primitive that allows threads to wait for an event to occur

118.   Answer: The Semaphore class is used to control access to a resource by a fixed number of threads.

119.   Answer: The Barrier class is used to synchronize a fixed number of threads at a specific point, where each thread must wait until all other threads have reached the barrier.

120.   Answer: The Timer class is used to schedule a function to be executed after a specified delay.

121.   Answer: The ThreadLocal class is used to create thread-

local data, where each thread has its own private copy of the data.

122.   Answer: The concurrent.futures module provides a high-level interface for asynchronously executing callables and managing their results.

123.   Answer: The ProcessPoolExecutor class is used to asynchronously execute callables in a sepa

124.   Answer: The ThreadPoolExecutor class is used to asynchronously execute callables in a thread pool.

125.   Answer: The Future class represents the result of a

computation that may not have completed yet.

126.   Answer: The concurrent.futures.as_completed () function is used to iterate over a sequence of futures as they complete.

127.   Answer: The concurrent.futures.wait() function is used to wait for a set of futures to complete.

128.   Answer: In the context of database programming, a context is a set of operations that are executed atomically, meaning they are either all committed or all rolled back.

129.   Answer: The sqlite3 module provides a way to interact with SQLite databases using Python.

130.   Answer: You can connect to an SQLite database in Python using the sqlite3.connect() function.

131.   Answer: In the context of database programming, a cursor is an object used to execute SQL statements and retrieve results from a database.

132.   Answer: The execute() method of a cursor is used to execute an SQL statement or a parameterized SQL statement.

133.   fetchone() method of a cursor is used to retrieve the next row of a query result set.

134.   Answer: The fetchall() method of a cursor is used to retrieve all remaining rows of a query result set

135.   Answer: The fetchmany() method of a cursor is used to retrieve a specific number of rows from a query result set.

136.   Answer: The commit() method is used to save changes made in a transaction to the database.

137.   Answer: The rollback() method is used to discard changes made in a transaction and roll back to the previous state.

138.   Answer: The psycopg2 module is a PostgreSQL adapter

for Python, which allows Python programs to access PostgreSQL databases.

139.   Answer: You can connect to a PostgreSQL database in Python using the psycopg2.connect() function.

140.   Answer: The MySQLdb module is a MySQL adapter for Python, which allows Python programs to access MySQL databases.

141.   Answer: You can connect to a MySQL database in Python using the MySQLdb.connect() function.

142.   Answer: The pyodbc module is an open-source Python module that allows Python programs to

access databases using the ODBC (Open Database Connectivity) standard.

143.   Answer: You can connect to a database using pyodbc by creating a connection string and passing it to the pyodbc.connect() function.

144.   Answer: The requests module is a popular third-party library for making HTTP requests in Python.

145.   Answer: You can make an HTTP GET request using the requests.get() function.

146.   Answer: You can make an HTTP POST request using the requests.post() function.

147. Answer: The response object represents the server's response to an HTTP request and provides access to the response headers, content, and status code.

148. Answer: Web scraping is the process of automatically extracting data from websites by sending HTTP requests, parsing the HTML response, and extracting the desired information.

149. Answer: The BeautifulSoup library is a popular third-party library for parsing HTML and XML documents.

150. Answer: You can parse an HTML document using BeautifulSoup by creating a

BeautifulSoup object and passing the HTML content and a parser as arguments.

151.   Answer: The find() method is used to find the first occurrence of a tag or a set of tags in an HTML document.

152.   Answer: The find_all() method is used to find all occurrences of a tag or a set of tags in an HTML document.

153.   Answer: The select() method is used to find elements in an HTML document using CSS selectors.

154.   Answer: The json module provides methods for working with JSON (JavaScript Object

Notation) data, including serialization and deserialization.

155.   Answer: You can serialize a Python object to JSON using the json.dumps() function.

156.   Answer: You can deserialize JSON to a Python object using the json.loads() function.

157.   Answer: The unittest module provides a framework for writing and running tests in Python.

158.   Answer: You can define a test case by creating a subclass of the unittest.TestCase class and defining test methods that start with the prefix test_.

159.   Answer: The setUp() method is called before each test method

in a test case and is used to set up the test environment.

160.   Answer: The tearDown() method is called after each test method in a test case and is used to clean up the test environment.

161.   Answer: The assertEqual() method is used to assert that two values are equal.

162.   Answer: The assertTrue() method is used to assert that a given condition is true.

163.   Answer: The assertFalse() method is used to assert that a given condition is false.

164.   Answer: The assertRaises() method is used to assert that a specified exception is raised when executing a given callable.

165.   Answer: The mock module provides tools for replacing parts of your system under test with mock objects.

166.   Answer: Mocking is a technique used in testing to replace real objects with fake or mock objects in order to isolate and control the behavior of the system under test.

167.   Answer: The patch() function is used to temporarily replace an object with a mock object during the execution of a test.

168.   Answer: The MagicMock class is a subclass of Mock that provides additional "magic" methods that allow you to

specify the behavior of the mock object.

169.　Answer: The patch.object() function is used to patch a specific attribute or method of an object with a mock object.

170.　Answer: The patch.dict() function is used to temporarily replace a dictionary with a mock dictionary during the execution of a test.

171.　Answer: The patch.multiple() function is used to patch multiple attributes or methods of an object with mock objects.

172.　Answer: The patch.context() function is used to patch an object for the duration of a context manager.

173.   Answer: The patch.dict() function is used to temporarily replace a dictionary with a mock dictionary during the execution of a test.

174.   Answer: The patch.multiple() function is used to patch multiple attributes or methods of an object with mock objects.

175.   Answer: The patch.context() function is used to patch an object for the duration of a context manager.

176.   Answer: The numpy module is a powerful library for numerical computing in Python,

providing support for large, multi-dimensional arrays and matrices, along with a collection of mathematical functions.

177.   Answer: A NumPy array is a data structure that represents a multi-dimensional, homogeneous array of fixed-size items.

178.   Answer: You can create a NumPy array using the numpy.array() function and passing a sequence-like object as an argument.

179.   Answer: The shape attribute of a NumPy array returns a tuple that represents the dimensions of the array.

180. Answer: The dtype attribute of a NumPy array returns the data type of the array.

181. Answer: You can perform mathematical operations on NumPy arrays using arithmetic operators or NumPy's mathematical functions.

182. Answer: The numpy.random module provides functions for generating random numbers and random arrays.

183. Answer: You can generate random numbers using functions such as numpy.random.rand(), numpy.random.randint(), or numpy.random.normal().

184. Answer: The numpy.arange() function is used

to create an array with evenly spaced values within a specified range.

185.   Answer: The numpy.linspace() function is used to create an array with a specified number of evenly spaced values within a specified range.

186.   Answer: The numpy.reshape() function is used to change the shape of a NumPy array without changing its data.

187.   Answer: The numpy.transpose() function is used to reverse or permute the axes of a NumPy array.

188.   Answer: The numpy.concatenate() function is

used to join two or more arrays along an existing axis.

189.   Answer: The numpy.split() function is used to split an array into multiple sub-arrays along a specified axis.

190.   Answer: The numpy.max() function is used to find the maximum value in an array.

191.   Answer: The numpy.min() function is used to find the minimum value in an array.

192.   Answer: The numpy.mean() function is used to calculate the arithmetic mean of an array.

193.   Answer: The numpy.median() function is used to calculate the median value of an array.

194.   Answer: The numpy.sum() function is used to calculate the sum of the elements in an array.

195.   Answer: The numpy.prod() function is used to calculate the product of the elements in an array.

196.   Answer: The numpy.dot() function is used to calculate the dot product of two arrays.

197.   Answer: The numpy.vstack() function is used to stack arrays vertically (row-wise).

198.   Answer: The numpy.hstack() function is used to stack arrays horizontally (column-wise).

199.   Answer: The numpy.random.seed() function is used to set the seed of the

random number generator in NumPy.

200.   Answer: The pandas library is a powerful library for data manipulation and analysis in Python, providing data structures and functions for efficiently working with structured data.

201.   Answer: A DataFrame is a two-dimensional, labeled data structure in the pandas library that represents a table of rows and columns.

202.   Answer: You can create a DataFrame in pandas by passing a dictionary, a list of dictionaries, or a NumPy array as an argument to the pandas.DataFrame() constructor.

203. Answer: The head() method is used to return the first n rows of a DataFrame.

204. Answer: The tail() method is used to return the last n rows of a DataFrame.

205. Answer: The shape attribute of a DataFrame returns a tuple that represents the dimensions (number of rows and columns) of the DataFrame.

206. Answer: The columns attribute of a DataFrame returns an Index object that represents the column labels of the DataFrame.

207. Answer: The index attribute of a DataFrame returns an Index

object that represents the row labels of the DataFrame.

208.   Answer: The info() method is used to display a concise summary of a DataFrame, including the column names, data types, and memory usage.

209.   Answer: The describe() method is used to generate descriptive statistics of a DataFrame, such as count, mean, standard deviation, minimum, maximum, and quartiles.

210.   Answer: The iloc[] indexer is used to select rows and columns of a DataFrame by their integer positions.

211.　Answer: The loc[] indexer is used to select rows and columns of a DataFrame by their labels.

212.　Answer: The [] operator is a versatile indexer in pandas that can be used to select columns, rows, or subsets of a DataFrame based on different criteria.

213.　Answer: The dropna() method is used to remove rows or columns from a DataFrame that contain missing values (NaN).

214.　Answer: The fillna() method is used to fill missing values (NaN) in a DataFrame with a specified value or using a predefined method.

215. Answer: The groupby() method is used to group rows of a DataFrame based on one or more columns, allowing for aggregate functions to be applied to each group.

216. Answer: The apply() method is used to apply a function to each row or column of a DataFrame, allowing for custom transformations.

217. Answer: The merge() function is used to merge two or more DataFrames based on common columns or indices.

218. Answer: The concat() function is used to concatenate two or more DataFrames along a specified axis.

219. Answer: The read_csv() function is used to read data from a CSV file and create a DataFrame.

220. Answer: The to_csv() method is used to write a DataFrame to a CSV file.

221. Answer: The matplotlib library is a popular plotting library for creating static, animated, and interactive visualizations in Python.

222. Answer: You can create a line plot using the matplotlib.pyplot.plot() function and passing the x and y values as arguments.

223. Answer: You can create a scatter plot using the

matplotlib.pyplot.scatter() function and passing the x and y values as arguments.

224.   Answer: You can create a bar plot using the matplotlib.pyplot.bar() function and passing the x and y values as arguments.

225.   Answer: You can create a histogram using the matplotlib.pyplot.hist() function and passing the data values as an argument.

226.   Answer: You can create a pie chart using the matplotlib.pyplot.pie() function and passing the data values as an argument.

227. Answer: You can add labels and titles to a plot using functions such as matplotlib.pyplot.xlabel(), matplotlib.pyplot.ylabel(), and matplotlib.pyplot.title().

228. Answer: The seaborn library is a statistical data visualization library based on matplotlib, providing a higher-level interface for creating informative and attractive statistical graphics.

229. Answer: You can create a box plot using the seaborn.boxplot() function and passing the data values and optional parameters as arguments.

230. Answer: You can create a violin plot using the

seaborn.violinplot() function and passing the data values and optional parameters as arguments.

231.   Answer: You can create a heatmap using the seaborn.heatmap() function and passing the data values and optional parameters as arguments.

232.   Answer: You can create a pair plot using the seaborn.pairplot() function and passing a DataFrame or an array-like object as an argument.

233.   Answer: The scikit-learn library is a popular machine learning library in Python that provides tools for data

preprocessing, modeling, and evaluation.

234.   Answer: Supervised learning is a machine learning technique where a model is trained using labeled examples (input-output pairs) to make predictions or classify new, unseen data.

235.   Answer: Unsupervised learning is a machine learning technique where a model is trained using unlabeled data to discover patterns or structures in the data.

236.   Answer: The fit() method is used to train a model on a given dataset.

237.   Answer: The predict() method is used to make

predictions or classifications on new, unseen data using a trained model.

238.   Answer: The transform() method is used to apply a transformation to a dataset, such as feature scaling or dimensionality reduction.

239.   Answer: The score() method is used to evaluate the performance of a model on a given dataset.

240.   ? Answer: The train_test_split() function is used to split a dataset into training and testing sets for model evaluation.

241.   Answer: The cross_val_score() function is used

to perform cross-validation and obtain the performance scores of a model on different subsets of the data.

242. Answer: The KMeans class is used to perform K-means clustering, a popular unsupervised learning algorithm for clustering data into K distinct groups.

243. Answer: The DecisionTreeClassifier class is used to perform classification using decision trees, a supervised learning algorithm that builds a tree-like model of decisions and their possible consequences.

244. Answer: The RandomForestClassifier class is used to perform classification

using random forests, an ensemble learning method that combines multiple decision trees to improve predictive accuracy and reduce overfitting.

245. Answer: The LinearRegression class is used to perform linear regression, a supervised learning algorithm for modeling the relationship between a dependent variable and one or more independent variables.

246. Answer: The LogisticRegression class is used to perform logistic regression, a supervised learning algorithm used for binary classification or estimating probabilities.

247.   Answer: The metrics module provides functions for evaluating the performance of models, including accuracy, precision, recall, F1-score, and more.

248.   Answer: The thread module provides a lower-level interface for creating and managing threads in Python.

249.

```
def longest_increasing_subsequence(arr):

    n = len(arr)

    dp = [1] * n

    for i in range(1, n):

        for j in range(i):

            if arr[i] > arr[j] and dp[i] < dp[j] + 1:
```

250. **Answer: You can convert a string to a list in Python by using the split() method. The split() method splits a string into a list of substrings based on a specified delimiter. By default, the delimiter is a whitespace.**

QUESTIONS BELOW

1. What is Python?

2. What is PEP 8?

3. What is a Python package?

4. What is the difference between a list and a tuple in Python?

5. What is a lambda function in Python?

6. What is the purpose of the if __name__ == "__main__" statement in Python?

7. What is the difference between == and is operators in Python?

8. How can you copy an object in Python?

9. What is the purpose of the __init__ method in Python classes?

10.   What is the difference between a shallow copy and a deep copy?

11.   What is the purpose of the super() function in Python?

12.   How can you handle exceptions in Python?

13.   What is a generator function in Python?

14.   What is the Global Interpreter Lock (GIL) in Python?

15.   What is the purpose of the yield keyword in Python?

16.   What are the built-in data types in Python?

17.   How can you open and read a file in Python?

18.   What is the purpose of the with statement in Python?

19.   What is the difference between append() and extend() methods of a list in Python?

20. How can you iterate over a dictionary in Python?

21. What is the purpose of the pass statement in Python?

22. How can you reverse a string in Python?

23. What is the purpose of the range() function in Python?

24. What is the purpose of the break statement in Python?

25. What is the purpose of the continue statement in Python?

26. What is the difference between a shallow copy and a deep copy of a list in Python?

27.   How can you remove duplicate elements from a list in Python?

28.   How can you find the index of an element in a list in Python?

29.   What is the purpose of the join() method in Python?

30.   What is the purpose of the format() method in Python strings?

31.   What is the purpose of the strip() method in Python strings?

32.   What is the purpose of the replace() method in Python strings?

33. What is the purpose of the split() method in Python strings?

34. What is a decorator in Python?

35. What is the purpose of the staticmethod decorator in Python?

36. What is the purpose of the classmethod decorator in Python?

37. What is a module in Python?

38. What is the purpose of the __name__ variable in Python?

39. What is the purpose of the sys module in Python?

40.   What is the purpose of the os module in Python?

41.   How can you check if a file exists in Python?

42.   What is the purpose of the pickle module in Python?

43.   What is the purpose of the json module in Python?

44.   What is the purpose of the datetime module in Python?

45.   What is the purpose of the random module in Python?

46.   What is the purpose of the time module in Python?

47.   What is the purpose of the re module in Python?

48.   What is the purpose of the collections module in Python?

49.   What is the purpose of the itertools module in Python?

50.   What is the purpose of the unittest module in Python?

51.   What is a docstring in Python?

52.   How can you access command-line arguments in Python?

53.   What is the purpose of the sys.exit() function in Python?

54.   What is the purpose of the os.path module in Python?

55.   What is the purpose of the os.getcwd() function in Python?

56.   What is the purpose of the os.chdir() function in Python? What is the purpose of the os.listdir() function in Python?

57.   What is the purpose of the os.mkdir() function in Python?

58.   What is the purpose of the os.rmdir() function in Python?

59.   What is the purpose of the os.remove() function in Python?

60. What is the purpose of the os.rename() function in Python?

61. What is the purpose of the os.path.isfile() function in Python?

62. What is the purpose of the os.path.isdir() function in Python?

63. What is the purpose of the os.path.exists() function in Python?

64. What is the purpose of the os.path.join() function in Python?

65.   What is the purpose of the os.path.splitext() function in Python?

66.   What is the purpose of the os.path.dirname() function in Python?

67.   What is the purpose of the os.path.basename() function in Python?

68.   What is the purpose of the os.path.getsize() function in Python?

69.   What is the purpose of the os.path.getmtime() function in Python?

70. What is the purpose of the os.environ dictionary in Python?

71. What is the purpose of the os.path.expanduser() function in Python?

72. What is the purpose of the os.path.expandvars() function in Python?

73. What is the purpose of the os.path.abspath() function in Python?

74. What is the purpose of the os.path.normpath() function in Python?

75.   What is the purpose of the os.path.relpath() function in Python?

76.   What is the purpose of the os.path.commonpath() function in Python?

77.   What is a context manager in Python?

78.   How can you define a context manager in Python?

79.   What is the purpose of the yield statement in a context manager?

80. What is the purpose of the __enter__() method in a context manager?

81. What is the purpose of the __exit__() method in a context manager?

82. What is the purpose of the @contextmanager decorator in Python?

83. What is the purpose of the try statement in Python?

84. What is the purpose of the except statement in Python?

85. What is the purpose of the finally statement in Python?

86. What is the purpose of the else statement in a try block in Python?

87. What is an exception in Python?

88. What is an error in Python?

89. What is the purpose of the raise statement in Python?

90. What is the purpose of the assert statement in Python?

91. What is an iterator in Python?

92. What is the purpose of the iter() function in Python?

93. What is the purpose of the next() function in Python?

94. What is the purpose of the StopIteration exception in Python?

95. What is a generator in Python?

96. What is the purpose of the yield statement in a generator?

97. What is the difference between a generator and a regular function in Python?

98. What is a coroutine in Python?

99.   What is the purpose of the async keyword in Python?

100.   What is the purpose of the await keyword in Python?

101.   What is an asynchronous generator in Python?

102.   What is the purpose of the asyncio module in Python?

103.   What is an event loop in Python asyncio?

104.   What is a task in Python asyncio?

105.   What is a future in Python asyncio?

106. What is the purpose of the async with statement in Python?

107. What is the purpose of the async for statement in Python? What is the purpose of the asyncio.sleep() function in Python? Answer: The asyncio.sleep() function is used to pause the execution of a coroutine for a specified amount of time.

108. What is a thread in Python?

109. What is the purpose of the threading module in Python?

110. **What is the Global Interpreter Lock (GIL) in Python?**

111. **What is the purpose of the threading.Thread class in Python?**

112. **What is a thread-safe object in Python?**

113. **What is a race condition in multithreaded programming?**

114. **What is the purpose of the Lock class in Python threading?**

115. **What is the purpose of the RLock class in Python threading?**

116. What is the purpose of the Condition class in Python threading?

117. What is the purpose of the Event class in Python threading?.

118. What is the purpose of the Semaphore class in Python threading?

119. What is the purpose of the Barrier class in Python threading?

120. What is the purpose of the Timer class in Python threading?

121. What is the purpose of the ThreadLocal class in Python threading?

122. What is the purpose of the concurrent.futures module in Python?

123. What is the purpose of the ProcessPoolExecutor class in concurrent.futures? rate process pool.

124. What is the purpose of the ThreadPoolExecutor class in concurrent.futures?

125. What is the purpose of the concurrent.futures.Future class?

126. What is the purpose of the concurrent.futures.as_completed () function?

127. **What is the purpose of the concurrent.futures.wait() function?**

128. **What is a context in the context of database programming?**

129. **What is the purpose of the sqlite3 module in Python?**

130. **How can you connect to an SQLite database in Python?**

131. **What is a cursor in the context of database programming?**

132. What is the purpose of the execute() method of a cursor in Python?

133. What is the purpose of the fetchone() method of a cursor in Python?

134. The What is the purpose of the fetchall() method of a cursor in Python?.

135. What is the purpose of the fetchmany() method of a cursor in Python?

136. What is the purpose of the commit() method in Python database programming?

137. What is the purpose of the rollback() method in Python database programming?

138. What is the purpose of the psycopg2 module in Python?

139. How can you connect to a PostgreSQL database in Python using psycopg2?

140. What is the purpose of the MySQLdb module in Python?

141. How can you connect to a MySQL database in Python using MySQLdb?

142. What is the purpose of the pyodbc module in Python?

143. How can you connect to a database using pyodbc?

144. What is the purpose of the requests module in Python?

145. How can you make an HTTP GET request using the requests module?

146. How can you make an HTTP POST request using the requests module?

147. What is the purpose of the response object returned by the requests module?

148. What is a web scraping in Python?

149. What is the purpose of the BeautifulSoup library in Python?

150. How can you parse an HTML document using BeautifulSoup?

151. What is the purpose of the find() method in BeautifulSoup?

152. What is the purpose of the find_all() method in BeautifulSoup?

153. What is the purpose of the select() method in BeautifulSoup?

154. What is the purpose of the json module in Python?

155.   How can you serialize a Python object to JSON using the json module?

156.   How can you deserialize JSON to a Python object using the json module?

157.   What is the purpose of the unittest module in Python?

158.   How can you define a test case using the unittest module?

159.   What is the purpose of the setUp() method in the unittest module?

160. What is the purpose of the tearDown() method in the unittest module?

161. What is the purpose of the assertEqual() method in the unittest module?

162. What is the purpose of the assertTrue() method in the unittest module?

163. What is the purpose of the assertFalse() method in the unittest module?

164. What is the purpose of the assertRaises() method in the unittest module?

165. What is the purpose of the mock module in Python?

166. What is mocking in Python?

167. What is the purpose of the patch() function in the mock module?

168. What is the purpose of the MagicMock class in the mock module?

169. What is the purpose of the patch.object() function in the mock module?

170. What is the purpose of the patch.dict() function in the mock module?

171. What is the purpose of the patch.multiple() function in the mock module?

172. What is the purpose of the patch.context() function in the mock module?

173. What is the purpose of the patch.dict() function in the mock module?

174. What is the purpose of the patch.multiple() function in the mock module?

175. What is the purpose of the patch.context() function in the mock module?

176.   What is the purpose of the numpy module in Python?

177.   What is a NumPy array in Python?

178.   How can you create a NumPy array in Python?

179.   What is the purpose of the shape attribute of a NumPy array?

180.   What is the purpose of the dtype attribute of a NumPy array?

181.   How can you perform mathematical operations on NumPy arrays in Python?

182.　What is the purpose of the numpy.random module in Python?

183.　How can you generate random numbers using the numpy.random module?

184.　What is the purpose of the numpy.arange() function?

185.　What is the purpose of the numpy.linspace() function?

186.　What is the purpose of the numpy.reshape() function?

187.　What is the purpose of the numpy.transpose() function?

188. What is the purpose of the numpy.concatenate() function?

189. What is the purpose of the numpy.split() function?

190. What is the purpose of the numpy.max() function?

191. What is the purpose of the numpy.min() function?

192. What is the purpose of the numpy.mean() function?

193. What is the purpose of the numpy.median() function?

194. What is the purpose of the numpy.sum() function?

195. What is the purpose of the numpy.prod() function?

196. What is the purpose of the numpy.dot() function?

197. What is the purpose of the numpy.vstack() function?

198. What is the purpose of the numpy.hstack() function?

199. What is the purpose of the numpy.random.seed() function?

200. What is the purpose of the pandas library in Python?

201. What is a DataFrame in the context of the pandas library?

202. How can you create a DataFrame in pandas?

203. What is the purpose of the head() method in pandas?

204. What is the purpose of the tail() method in pandas?

205. What is the purpose of the shape attribute of a DataFrame in pandas?

206. What is the purpose of the columns attribute of a DataFrame in pandas

207. What is the purpose of the index attribute of a DataFrame in pandas?

208. What is the purpose of the info() method in pandas?

209. What is the purpose of the describe() method in pandas?

210. What is the purpose of the iloc[] indexer in pandas?

211. What is the purpose of the loc[] indexer in pandas?

212. What is the purpose of the [] operator in pandas?

213. What is the purpose of the dropna() method in pandas?

214. What is the purpose of the fillna() method in pandas?

215. What is the purpose of the groupby() method in pandas?

216. What is the purpose of the apply() method in pandas?

217. What is the purpose of the merge() function in pandas?

218. What is the purpose of the concat() function in pandas?

219. What is the purpose of the read_csv() function in pandas?

220. What is the purpose of the to_csv() method in pandas?

221. What is the purpose of the matplotlib library in Python?

222.   How can you create a line plot using matplotlib?

223.   How can you create a scatter plot using matplotlib?

224.   How can you create a bar plot using matplotlib?

225.   How can you create a histogram using matplotlib?

226.   How can you create a pie chart using matplotlib?

227.   How can you add labels and titles to a plot using matplotlib?

228.   What is the purpose of the seaborn library in Python?

229. How can you create a box plot using seaborn?

230. How can you create a violin plot using seaborn?

231. How can you create a heatmap using seaborn?

232. How can you create a pair plot using seaborn?

233. What is the purpose of the scikit-learn library in Python?

234. What is supervised learning in machine learning?

235. What is unsupervised learning in machine learning?

236. What is the purpose of the fit() method in scikit-learn?

237. What is the purpose of the predict() method in scikit-learn?

238. What is the purpose of the transform() method in scikit-learn?

239. What is the purpose of the score() method in scikit-learn?

240. What is the purpose of the train_test_split() function in scikit-learn?

241. What is the purpose of the cross_val_score() function in scikit-learn?

242. What is the purpose of the KMeans class in scikit-learn?

243. What is the purpose of the DecisionTreeClassifier class in scikit-learn?

244. What is the purpose of the RandomForestClassifier class in scikit-learn?

245. What is the purpose of the LinearRegression class in scikit-learn?

246. What is the purpose of the LogisticRegression class in scikit-learn?

247. What is the purpose of the metrics module in scikit-learn?

248. What is the purpose of the thread module in Python?

249. Implement a function to find the longest increasing subsequence in an array of integers. The subsequence does not have to be contiguous.

250. How can you convert a string to a list in Python?